Shout for Joy

poems from the journey

Sharina Smith
www.sharinasmith.com

Copyright © 2004 by Sharina Smith

Shout For Joy
by Sharina Smith

Printed in the United States of America

ISBN 1-594673-22-5

All rights reserved by the author. The contents and views expressed in this book are solely those of the author and are not necessarily those of Xulon Press, Inc. The author guarantees this book is original and does not infringe upon any laws or rights, and that this book is not libelous, plagiarized or in any other way illegal. If any portion of this book is fictitious, the author guarantees it does not represent any real event or person in a way that could be deemed libelous. No part of this book may be reproduced in any form without the permission of the author.

Unless otherwise indicated, Bible quotations are taken from *NIV Women of Faith Study Bible*, *New International Version*. Copyright ©2001 by The Zondervan Corporation.

the unbearable lightness of being was first published in *Forum*, Bliss Station Publishing, 2001. *excuse me* was first published in *The Business Women's Advantage*, Mershon Bell, 2001.

Dedication

To Chuck, my best friend and first love,
thank you for enduring the long road back to me.

To Laura, Daniel, Jacob, and Adam,
I thank God for the privilege of being your
mother and stepmother.

But the angel said to them, "Do not be afraid, I bring you good news of great joy that will be for all the people. Today in the town of David a Savior has been born to you; he is Christ the Lord."
(Luke 2:10-11)

> *"In the Bible, joy is continually associated with a feeling of utter amazement and happiness associated with a true love of God. As Luke stated above, the greatest joy is the everlasting life offered by Christ. In almost every instance the word 'joy' is used in the Bible, it connotes singing, shouting, and proclaiming a deep feeling in one's heart—one that can be truly fulfilled only by a love of God."*

—Jonathan Niemeyer in *Harvesting Spiritual Fruit: Following God's Path to True Love, Joy and Peace*

Contents

Acknowledgements	xiii
Introduction: *The Journey*	xv

West Plains, Missouri 1978
The Mysteries of the Mind	28
Missouri Sunshine	29
Far Away	30
A Child's Prayer	31
the hour-glass	32

Memphis, Tennessee 1983
Madness	34
dirty angry people	35

West Plains, Missouri 1983
The house itself speaks of death	38

Bryn Mawr, Pennsylvania 1984 – 1986
from the Sketchbook I	40
from the Sketchbook II	41
A New Start	42
where are the voices	44
death drips dark	45

King of Prussia, Pennsylvania 1989
Life in the Mall	48
Separation Anxiety	49
I long for you	50
Crucify me	51

Can I mend	52
We all age	53
Where are my words tonight?	54

Philadelphia, Pennsylvania 1989-1992

Twenty-five	56
As I sit	57
What is missing	58
I am dying of boredom	59
Why this need for words?	60
Stagnant waters	61
Fire painting	62
No soul without love	63
The night is cool and dark	64
My greatest fear	65
My words comfort me tonight	66
No Touch	67
Amen	68
I. To the Pharmacy	69
II. To the Pharmacy	70
the unbearable lightness of being	71
I'm gonna laugh you outta my life	72
No expectations	73
Must I sit in the sunbeam?	74
I must be strong and wise	75
joie de vivre	76
A hopeful time	77
I. Ennui grips again	78
II. Ennui grips again	79
Stasis in darkness	80
Hanging On	81
I try to sing	82
Wailing virgins	83

God, it's late	84
Runaway	85
I feel too much now	86
Sweet wine symphony	87
Excuse me	88
Words of truth	89
The Birthing	90

Chester Springs, Pennsylvania 1992

An Orchid in the Arctic*

One careless footstep	92
No room for mystery and magic	92
There is a profound difference	93
It is so lonely in the Arctic	93
Orchids' Haven	94
Orchid Truth	94
I want to smear pink paint	95
The Holy Grail	96
little tiny shards of glass	97
Shattered	98
Wild women	99
A woman sings	100

West Plains, Missouri 1995

I am a new mother	102
Sylvia, I'm sorry	103
It's about time	104

West Plains, Missouri 1999

For the love of God	106
Were You There	107

West Plains, Missouri 2000
bad poetry — 110
the screen doesn't lie — 111
my heart is singing — 112
bliss bliss bliss — 113
melting — 114

West Plains, Missouri 2001
September 11, 2001 — 116
learning to love is just the beginning — 118

West Plains, Missouri 2002
but I am not God — 120
motherhood, millions, matters — 122
intentional life — 124
divorce — 126
aftermath — 127
glimmer of joy — 129

Springfield, Missouri 2003
thanks, God — 132
Daddy? — 134
die editor die — 136
thirty-nine — 137
shout for joy — 139

Bibliography and Notes — 141

About the Author — 143

Acknowledgements

The shout of pain leads to the shout of joy. I thank God for accompanying me on the journey. There are many people, places, and situations which have made this book possible. They all have played a part in my journey.

I am grateful for:

- my painful childhood, because I learned to endure.

- my brother, George, and his sweet family, because they, too, have endured.

- my teachers in West Plains, Missouri, because they taught me to read and write and sing, three of my greatest joys.

- the wealthy in the big city, because they provided funding for my higher education.

- the authors whose books are my friends, because they are there whenever I am lonely.

- the Ozarks, because its bittersweet landscape soothes my soul.

- Ridgecrest Baptist Church, because it gives me a loving place to work and worship, and loving people to share the journey. I especially want to thank the colleagues who were patient readers of this book.

- my husband's parents, Ed and Ruth, because they have taught me what it is like to have a loving dad and mom.

- my sister-in-law, Sherry, because we can laugh and cry together through anything.

- my children, Laura and Daniel, and my stepchildren, Jacob and Adam, because you teach me patience and you bring me great joy.

- my husband, Chuck, because you never forgot me and the love we shared. I love you for reading my book and being a terrific editor even though you don't "get" poetry. You really are my hero and best friend.

I am truly blessed.

And now begins the journey…

Introduction: The Journey

S*hout for Joy* has been a journey twenty-five years in the making. The journey began twenty-five years ago when I penned the first poem of this collection moments before I attempted suicide. I was 14 years old. My father had died just a few months before, and while I should have been rejoicing because I was finally free from his physical and sexual abuse, I was grieving. He was the parent I thought loved me. I think my suicide attempt was as much a cry for my mother to finally notice me and nurture me as it was an attempt to join my daddy in eternal rest. On that hot, summer night in 1978, I swallowed a bottle full of pills, wrote a poem, and waited for something to happen. I think I had passed in and out of consciousness a few times when my younger brother found me, and I yelled at him to go get our mother to help me. Instead of the newspaper headlines and ambulance sirens I had imagined upon my death, I received my mother's wrath.

After enduring a night of her forcing me to drink black coffee – her idea of a private stomach pumping which to this day makes the thought of black coffee nauseating for me – and her wailing about how now she couldn't trust me to go to high school in the fall because I was going to do drugs, I made a decision. I was going to show her. I would not do drugs. I would be valedictorian of my high school class and she would be proud of me instead of her usual disappointed state. I had just graduated from eighth grade as valedictorian, so my goal was not too far-fetched. I decided that God had made me cry out just before I passed out for a reason. I felt called to get an education and get out of town.

By the grace of God, I rose up out of the ashes of depression over daddy's death and I embarked upon my high school years. My high school mascot was a "Zizzer," and I soon became an example of a lightning bolt-like flash of light. What a joyful time! I lived with a two-fold purpose: 1) to get the best grades so I could prove to my mother I was more than a drug addict wanna-be and 2) to feel no pain. During my first two years of high school, I played basketball, sang in choir, and acted in plays. I perfected the art of burying my pain in busy-ness. By the time I was a senior, I was active in Concert Choir, Chamber Singers, and Girl Scouts; and I was an officer in the Drama Club, the Math and Science Club, Student Council, and the National Honor Society. At my church I was active in the youth group, sang in the adult choir, and directed the children's choir. As if that wasn't enough, in January of my senior year I agreed to help out my choir director and sing in the college choir she directed. Although I did not need one more activity, I think God had a hand in my joining the college choir.

The choir director at West Plains High School is like one of those teachers about whom movies are made. Kelly Dame is, in fact, still teaching there to this day, still inspiring a crowded room full of young country kids with an Ozark twang how to sing with the Queen's English. Her choir room was crowded and hot when 85 of us were in Concert Choir; I can only imagine what it is like now that the group nears 120. Kelly was not only a teacher to me. She was also a mentor and friend. We were neighbors and I spent many hours at her house babysitting and escaping my mother's drunk new husband. I thank Kelly for giving me the gift of a passion for music and for making it possible for me to meet the love of my life. My husband, Chuck Smith was a baritone in that college choir, but I first fell in love with his sister, Sherry, and her melodious laughter.

Sherry and I sang alto together and soon discovered we shared a twisted sense of humor. She and I would find something funny and sing with our shoulders shaking from nearly uncontrollable laughter. Her eyes would twinkle and I knew my own were returning the sparkle as we attempted to hold back our giggles. I especially loved the times in choir when we were arranged in a semi-circle because then I could stand next to Sherry's gorgeous younger brother, who unbeknownst to me had been secretly checking me out when we were standing in rows on the risers. After a couple months admiring her brother, I asked Sherry if she thought her brother might go to my senior prom with me. She smiled her mischievous smile and said she thought he might. After choir one night, I took a deep breath and invited Chuck to my prom. He said yes!

Before prom, Chuck and I spent time alone together getting to know each other over Sonic sodas. Prom night came and he looked devastatingly handsome in his powder blue tuxedo. His blue eyes were twinkling when he picked me up at my house. We went to his parents' house for them to admire us and take our picture. Before prom, Chuck had thoughtfully asked the color of my dress so he could buy me matching flowers. I wore white so his job of matching was made easy – the flowers he chose were beautiful. We enjoyed a lovely dinner together before prom, and we may have been in a high school gym, but I was in heaven dancing all night in his arms. After the dance we changed clothes and went to the school-sponsored post-prom drive in movie. I think the movie was "Zorro" but I spent more time kissing and being kissed by Chuck than watching the movie. I was in love. Unfortunately, I was also soon going far away.

Four years after my suicide attempt, I graduated as valedictorian of my high school class and left rural West Plains, Missouri for the big city. I was going to Bryn Mawr College thanks to the scholarship dollars my good grades had earned. After a bittersweet summer, I left behind my high school sweetheart and headed east. My journey took me far from the farm where I had milked goats, sheered sheep, and built barns in which my daddy took advantage of me. At Bryn Mawr, I learned to be a lady, learned to like alcohol, and learned how to read the great dead white males (as we fondly called them): Yeats, Milton, Ruskin, Whitman, Hawthorne and Hardy. It was also at Bryn Mawr that I discovered the legions of depressed women writers that came before me: Virginia Woolf, Sylvia Plath, Anne Sexton, Emily Dickinson, Jane Austen, and many more. Why did the writer women always have to die of suicide?

I was often depressed and wrote little poetry while at Bryn Mawr, but I had moments of joy despite working day and night to survive the academic challenges and the expense of staying in such a place. My beloved Gramma Clara sent joy in a box at least once a month when she sent her care packages full of fudge, cookies, and "snick snacks." She even sent me light reading as an antidote to the heavy tomes I toted around campus as an English and music major. My roommates and I howled at the *National Enquirer* headlines my grandmother wickedly packed in with the treats. Her homemade goodies soothed my soul. These regularly sent treats, coupled with the delicious cooking at Bryn Mawr, helped me discover the way to salvation through food. Enough food drowned the pain as much as alcohol, and I didn't have a hangover in the morning.

While at Bryn Mawr, I yearned to go back home, but my high school sweetheart found someone new, and I began my quest for the almighty dollar. Despite my scholarship and working three jobs, I was rapidly going into debt to pay for room, board, and books. There was a point at which I even contemplated prostitution to pay the bills, but odd jobs like babysitting always came up just in time. Although I stopped going to church when I moved east, I always felt the presence of a guardian angel in my life. I had loved going to the United Methodist Church back home as a little girl, especially when I sang in the choir, but I always felt out of place when I went to church in Bryn Mawr. Then I discovered the Episcopal Church paid singers and I was hooked. I became Episcopalian and supplemented my income without selling my soul.

After graduation, I went further into debt getting my first car and apartment, but I had a good job. While finishing up my senior year, I began working in marketing and public relations at the King of Prussia Mall, at that time the largest shopping center in the country. In the years that followed, I wandered from good job to good job, went in and out of debt, fell in and out of love, and drank away the pain still lingering in my heart. I attempted to fill a God-shaped void in my life with whiskey, wine, work, and song. Ten years out of high school, I looked good on paper. I had a great résumé: Bryn Mawr graduate; marketing, public relations, and fund raising expert; professional singer. I was enrolled in graduate school at West Chester University of Pennsylvania and engaged to marry a doctor. And my mother thought I would succumb to drugs. I had showed her. Unfortunately, she still wasn't proud of me.

With a masters degree in hand and a baby on the way, I began contemplating nice ways to make money. My counselor was also a massage therapist and so I enrolled in shiatsu school. My psychotherapist husband and I began dreaming of opening a clinic back in my home town to treat sexual abuse survivors. We moved and opened up a business together on Main Street. I was home. Our marriage had been dead when we moved, but I thought a change of scenery and a joint business venture would revive it. I was wrong. My husband grew closer to his patients and further away from me and our two small children. I found it difficult to make friends since I was so depressed and didn't want to be a burden on anyone. I went to therapy two times a week, refused antidepressants, drank just enough to numb the pain and ate even more. Just when I thought I'd never have close friends again, I ran into Chuck's sister Sherry in the post office one day and we rekindled our old friendship. She told me of her brother's failing marriage and she now says I sparkled, but I do not recall having such an obvious reaction. My first thought was to fix him up with another friend of mine, but I secretly longed for him to come and rescue me out of my miserable marriage. Too shy to ask Sherry where Chuck lived, I scanned the local phone book to see if I could find him.

Sherry brought so much joy back into my life when she invited me to join her in the community choir. After each rehearsal we renewed our friendship while talking in the parking lot. I slowly opened up to Sherry about my painful marriage and she told me about hers. I told her that singing had saved me when I was far away from home on the East Coast. Despite the disappointments of that time, I had made such wonderful friends singing in the Mendelssohn Club of Philadelphia, in various churches, and in a little opera company. Although many of my old singing friends were struggling to make it in the city, we had so much fun making music and enjoying meals together. When I first moved back to West Plains, I gave up singing and had forgotten how good it was to be surrounded by music and laughter. Thanks to Sherry and singing, I was starting to feel joy coming back in my life. Then, my mother suddenly died and after her death I lost everything else. One year later, her mother, my beloved Gramma Clara, died as well.

While my mother's death was devastating since she was only 58, my grandmother's death was after a good, long, well-lived life. Gramma Clara's funeral service was a special celebration because she had just accepted Christ after holding out for 91 years! I, too, had held out for several years not even knowing that I was truly loved by Jesus. Although I had sung the words and said the prayers in many Sundays at Church, I had never prayed the prayer of prayers until I realized that Jesus really loved me. Ironically enough, I accepted Christ in the final moments of a committee meeting on evangelism!

In March of 2002, I was on the board of MOPS (Mothers of Preschoolers) and we were discussing evangelism, when during our closing prayer, I broke down sobbing. All through the meeting I had been taking notes in the attempt to learn all I could about evangelism in the hopes that someday my husband would join me and our children in church. During the prayer, I realized that I had spent all my life trying to get my mother and then my husband to treasure me enough to come to church with me, while I didn't even believe that Jesus loved me. I loved church, but I couldn't even sing Jesus Loves Me to my children. I always sang, "Jesus loves you this I know," since the words, "Jesus loves me," were too painful. If Jesus loved me, why did He let my father abuse me and my mother not notice me? During the MOPS closing prayer, that question didn't matter anymore. I truly felt loved by Jesus, and in the presence of those sweet, godly mothers, I accepted Christ as my Lord and Savior. They put their lesson on evangelism to use that day!

Later that same year, it became clear my husband chose one of his former patients over fatherhood and marriage. He gave up his practice and filled his office with toys. Rooms full of his computers, pool tables, pianos, Legos*, and electric trains soon replaced my massage studio, self-help bookstore, and life coaching practice. I had finally found a nice way to make money and it fizzled in light of his lack of support. While still mourning my mother, I buried my marriage and my career. I had done some college teaching in West Plains, so I began substituting in local schools to pay the bills while I searched for a new career. Although my husband was the one to first abandon our marriage, I had been researching divorce myself and knew I needed another way to make money that was not so dependent upon my doctor husband.

The night before my husband asked for a divorce, God spoke to me and insisted I email my old high school sweetheart. I thought this heavenly urging was crazy, but I did have an email address for Chuck. After my mother had died, I had asked Sherry to forward an email newsletter I had written about my mother's life and death to her brother. Chuck wrote me a beautiful email of condolence and I kept his email address in my database. At the time, I had written him a note in return, but since he was in the midst of a divorce and I was still married, it felt wrong to continue a correspondence. I was sure emailing him a year later was crazy since email addresses change so often, but God's urging was insistent. I knew it was a God thing, because it didn't make any sense to email my old friend in the midst of my career dilemma. That night I didn't realize my husband was so seriously contemplating divorce, but I did realize that I had to have a little more money in the bank before I made any moves in that direction. Why I was prompted to write an old sweetheart about my career decision was not clear to me at the time. Now I know it was God's calling me to a new life. I was truly going home.

I emailed my old friend that night, woke up the next morning, took my kids to school and preschool, and went home to my husband who asked for a separation. Trying to be a good wife, I asked if he wanted to try counseling. He said that I was becoming too Christian for him and he could never see us rekindling our marriage. I asked if there was any hope. He said there was none. I said there was no point in him staying any longer since I knew he had already found someone new. He insisted that there wasn't anyone, but I knew. A woman always knows. He spent the next two days packing his things and each night went to his office to sleep after the kids went to bed. Two nights later we broke our children's hearts and told them we were getting a divorce. Their pain was almost more than I could bear even though I knew their father's leaving was freeing me from a 10-year prison. Looking back now, August 26, 2002 was my emancipation day. After enduring a long, cold marriage, my husband's abandoning our marriage vows freed me to complete the journey back to my old friend.

Meanwhile, Chuck had emailed me a return hello and we began corresponding. He was saddened at the news of my marriage ending and said he wanted to see me when he came to town. Sherry, too, had just been abandoned by her husband so I called and asked her if she wanted to get our children together for a Labor Day picnic. She said she couldn't since she didn't have her son that day and she was going up to Springfield to visit her brother. I told her I would call another single mom, but we'd get together soon. A few minutes later she called back. Sherry said Chuck wanted to invite me and my kids along for the day! While excited about seeing him, I was horrified at the thought of him seeing me, since I was 100 pounds heavier than I was 19 years earlier, and I had been crying all week over the death of my marriage. I decided if we were going to renew our friendship, I wanted him to see me at my worst. In anticipation of our reunion, I took our prom picture out of my high school yearbook where I had kept it all those years, and I tucked it into a book at my bedside. Looking at that picture of me in a beautiful white dress and him in his powder blue tuxedo, I prayed he would be my husband and I would be his wife this time.

Our reunion was so sweet. After all those years, he still looked like that 21-year old boy I had fallen in love with despite the gray hair and few pounds he had gained. I still felt fat but I could see he didn't care – he treated me like I was 18 and thin again. Despite what the divorce books all say, my children were eager to meet him and welcomed him into their life with open arms. With Sherry, we all spent one of the best days of my life walking in the woods, eating Sonic cheeseburgers, and shopping at Bass Pro. He had made us lovely omelets that morning and somehow got my coffee just the right mixture of sweetener and milk on the first try. That night he even got down in the floor with my children and played board games with them. I felt more married that day than I had ever been before. After that day, we began emailing each other regularly and, after our first phone call later that week, we began talking more and more frequently until we had our first date in 19 years. We ate steak, talked and laughed and kissed by the river in the moonlight. Although we weren't officially married until March 21, 2003, in my heart, September 21, 2002 was our wedding day. From that day forward, hardly a day went by when we did not speak to one another by telephone. Every few weeks we enjoyed spending time together in person.

Since he had never thought to give me his high school ring years ago, Chuck asked me to "go steady" and I wore his huge clunky ring proudly! Living 100 miles apart grew more and more difficult and we both agreed we would never want a long distance relationship again. On December 17, I knew I would leave Hemingway's Restaurant in Bass Pro Shop engaged to marry my old friend. I left our table to powder my nose and I noticed Mr. and Mrs. Santa eating dinner a few tables away – I was a little nervous Chuck would ask Santa to give me my ring! While I was gone, Chuck tucked a lovely sparkling engagement ring in a dinner roll and, upon my return, he offered me the bread basket. I refused until I saw one of the rolls had something in it. I laughed with relief that Santa wasn't going to be involved! With tears of regret in his eyes, Chuck asked the question he said he should have asked 19 years ago and proposed to me. With my own eyes filling with tears of joy, I accepted his proposal.

A week later on the night before Christmas Eve, I moved from West Plains to Springfield in the midst of a snowstorm and after settling my children into their new school and preschool, I began searching for a job. In the days before our wedding, I worked as a substitute teacher, made our house a home, and organized our wedding. Chuck ate supper with us most nights and taught me so much about taking care of my own children. What a difference having a good man at home to share the parenting! Although my children were hurting from the divorce and adjusting to a new level of discipline, they blossomed under the warmth of my soon-to-be husband's love. I began a relationship with my husband's children and fell in love with them. We began worshipping together at Ridgecrest Baptist Church and for the first time in 20 years, my old friend and I sang in choir together again. We had met in choir at school so long ago — what a joy to sing to the Lord with each other now!

With our four children in attendance and each playing a significant part in the ceremony, we enjoyed a beautiful wedding back home in West Plains. My new father-in-law gave me away. I could tell he was proud to escort me down the aisle to his son — he had kept a snapshot of his son and me on prom night in his jewelry box for 20 years and now he was walking me down the aisle at our wedding. Surrounded by many friends and family, we wed in the church of my youth. Although I had been Episcopalian since 1985, I had returned to my Methodist roots in 2002, and I had enjoyed a year singing and worshipping with old friends. The First United Methodist church choir sang at our wedding; some of the members had sung with me at the time I dated my new husband twenty years ago! The husband of the choir director who had first introduced us also sang for us. A circle was completed. Our prom picture graced the wedding program and we became man and wife.

It has been such a long road back home to Chuck. I can only imagine what our real home in heaven will be like, since I feel so safe and warm in the shelter of my husband's arms. Although the wounds of my childhood, our past career disappointments, and our difficult years apart have not fully healed, we are hopeful for the future. I enjoy my passion for writing while working fulltime at our church in the worship and music ministry, and although Chuck is grateful for a good job in corporate customer service, he dreams of finding work that allows him more time to indulge his passions for guns and hunting. While neither Chuck nor I would encourage anyone to begin a new marriage so soon after ending an old one, for us, the timing was perfect because it was God's timing. We were called to continue a friendship we had started many years ago. In fact, we had stopped dating at the end of August when I left for college, and we resumed dating 20 years later in September as if all those years hadn't passed. Our reunion was simply a miracle.

As we struggle to blend our family and negotiate with our ex-spouses, we daily regret not having married long ago. We reap the consequences of what we now know was our ignoring God's plan for us. I knew years ago I would enjoy being my husband's wife, but I selfishly followed my dreams of a fancy education and left him for the big city. He admits he has always loved me but was afraid I would regret living with him in the country if I didn't have an adventure in the big city. I was too proud to tell him when I was ready to come home after a year away. We both married other people despite God's warning signs. Our journey has taught us the importance of seeking God's will first. We daily give thanks for being given a second chance. We daily give thanks for the blessing of our marriage and the blessing of our children. When life is difficult, I often forget that God is still good, and I shout in search of joy, shaking my fist at Him for allowing bad things to happen to me and my family. When I finally remember all He has done for us, I raise my hands and shout for joy, thanking Him for His many blessings.

I hope that my journey will be an encouragement to you on yours. I firmly believe that I have survived to tell you my story because it has been the stories of other survivors that have motivated me to live. When I have been in the depths of depression and loneliness, it has been the poems and stories from the Bible and from the many books I have read that have encouraged me. Stories have brought me moments of joy in the midst of great pain. They have been my friends when I didn't feel I had any. I think it is no accident that Christ is the Word made flesh. Words are what seem to make us human, and as books have always been to me, Christ is our friend, especially when we feel most alone. All human life struggles to learn to speak. I hope my story speaks to you. I look forward to reading yours.

West Plains, Missouri

1978

Be happy young man, while you are young, and let your heart give you joy in the days of your youth.
(Ecclesiastes 11:9)

The Mysteries of the Mind

The mysteries of the mind are ours to unravel.
Is it possible to reveal the truth?
What lies in the deep?
Is it too sacred to fool with?
Will we ever know; should we want to know
The great secrets inside —
Memories of good times
Dreams of the future
— What lies behind these thoughts?
Ah, the great treasures there to be unfolded,
Shall we ever know their value?
Can they be appraised?
(The careless days of youth are treasured there;
 The feelings of growing up are held in pain there.)
Is it right that we should try to solve the mystery?
Something says not to ask, but just to accept.

I shall try.

Missouri Sunshine

I had never tasted caviar, drank champagne,
or sailed a yacht before,
But now as I do these things, they seem unimportant to me
Oh, I long for the Missouri Sunshine I once knew

The days went by too fast for me, the future came to quick
I still remember the fun we had and the times we shared,
Oh, where did the Missouri Sunshine go?

The friends and foes I once knew don't remember me,
The family has long since gone
The Missouri Sunshine let me go, oh so far away.

Now in a cold, lonely city I stay
Thinkin' of how times have changed
Missouri, why don't you come back to me?

Why I left the place I loved, I will never know
I long for the sunshine to warm my soul
Oh, Missouri please take me home.

Everyone has gone away; nothing is the same
Now all I have are sweet memories,
Of Missouri Sunshine I once knew.

Far Away

Far away out there
Is a wonderland
Where peace is present
Troubles are few
Yes...
I will go there
To seek the happiness
That I have not seen
For a long, long time
But...
Will I find this place
Does it exist only in my dreams
Shall I wish upon a star
Or must I hope in vain
No...
I will not find happiness
Only by dreaming or wishing
I must strive to make it be
But oh, it is so far away

A Child's Prayer

Lord, help me to believe in things
That I do not see or hear

Lord, forgive me when I do wrong
For I know that I have sinned

Lord, help me find the way
Let me see the light

Lord, give me strength when I am weak
For I know that thou art strong

Lord, help me realize that life isn't always easy
Please lead the way for me

Amen

the hour-glass

We are but grains of sand

f
  a
    l
      l
        i
          n
            g
    t
      h
        r
          o
            u
              g
                h

the hour-glass of time.

MEMPHIS, TENNESSEE

1983

A fool gives full vent to his anger, but a wise man keeps himself under control.
(Proverbs 29:11)

Madness

Madness eats away
like a saw
sawing, sawing
gnawing, gnawing
away at my heart
like a saw growing colder
while hotter, hotter
      so hot
      so mad
      so alone
in madness
Terrible hot tears
tremulous lips
heaving sighs
all held within
the inner being
The saw cuts deeper
until all is sawed
gnawed, sawed
all is sawed
Fearing all worlds apart
from the one
the one within
which is the most fearful
the most feared
the one mad

dirty angry people

So many people
    all angry
    all dirty
    all alone
Too many people
    surround me
    me
    all angry
    all dirty
    all alone
Dirty Angry People
People Dirty Angry
    Me
    Alone
    Surrounded
    Angry
    Alone
    Me

West Plains, Missouri

1983

*For with much wisdom comes much sorrow;
the more knowledge, the more grief.*
(Ecclesiastes 1:18)

The house itself speaks of death

The house itself speaks of death
I had fancied myself about to die
As if I were one so fortunate to be gone.
Not wishing dead, wishing gone.

The music swirls around me
Enveloping the cold, dark me
within the warmth so new.
Hands beat time as the pulse
        quickens the fevered heart.

The questioning one grows cold
As if all else were lost.
So happy yet so unsure
of self, of womanhood, of herself.

All was well and yet all was unwell.
A life of paradoxes loomed before her
As she struggled with the
truths passing before her.

Not wishing dead, wishing gone.
Yet these lips form around
        death as if to greet her
            with a kiss.

Bryn Mawr, Pennsylvania

1984–1986

Yet I hold this against you:
you have forsaken your first love.
(Rev. 2:4b)

from the Sketchbook I

In ways that cannot be mentioned
the visual conception
of reality is such that
All comes to one in a tizzying whirl
of delight,
or is it horror?
Vast and true — it is love.

Can it be that self-expression is
but an illusion of self-delusion?

from the Sketchbook II

Anger fades away
A momentary ecstasy finds its way
into the heart
Oh joy, my heart
Anger had wrenched you.

A New Start

So long away from my hand this pen
Like a babe starting to walk I cannot let go
Feel for the edge of the world
as I take a step
Towards what end do I resume climbing?

A new start
always requires courage
One cannot fail in our world
In my world
The words
will not
can not
attempt to restore
the missing elements
What is missing?
So long ago
asked many questions
many more
wait to be answered

So good to have you back again
You tumble forth from my pen
As if you were there all along
Aching to be spilled
Longing for release
Sweet and precious words

We are mere animals without you
We made you But you make us
Mere animal I am with you
Nobody knows my secret
I am a poet.

where are the voices

fragility of the age
no artists
no poets
no music
Where are the voices?

smeared paint
false Romantics
discordance,
fork on cat-gut scraped

no trust in self
no gods nor God
forsaken by Nature
Imagination not to be found
scream lady scream
my poem will do no better

death drips dark

death drips
dark
golden
drops
into the
chalice
the draught
is not
bitter
but
sickly, sickly
sweet
I drink
savoring
each
and every
taste
of pain
I lick my lips
reliving
the moment
of my
surrender
to death

King of Prussia, Pennsylvania

1989

Whoever loves money never has money enough;
whoever loves wealth is never satisfied with his income.
This too is meaningless.
(Ecclesiastes 5:10)

Life in the Mall

I live here
striving for
the almighty dollar.

I walk the mall
taking care
of business matters.

A woman hooks a rug while
muttering to herself.

Pizza, ice cream
eaten around her.

She's oblivious.

Separation Anxiety

write no poems
have no desires
dream no dreams

an experimental stage
brought upon by loss

Separation Anxiety
clinically described

am I better off (question mark understood)

I long for you

I trusted
      and lost
      at love

Mainstream desires
      you said
      I had

Severed are the ties
      that bound
      our love

Wasted dreams
      lost nights
      embracing no more

Mistaken love
      I long
      for you

Crucify me

a philosophy unfolding
love of God or of man
which is the true God
what or who do we worship
do we wear the cross for our
lust or our love of the spirit

crucify me

Can I mend

can I manage
can I mend
can I find meaning
can I fend
      for myself

We all age

can it be happiness?
and then there's Maude
      is she a *Designing Woman* now
      or merely a *Golden Girl*
we all age and find ourselves
      where we least expect to

Where are my words tonight?

where are my words tonight
    are the poems all gone
what means do I have for expressions
    through the men only
    wear the cross boldly
        if he says so
    take it off
        if he says so
    what is the true me
    where is she
can it be true
    that I am not true to myself?

Philadelphia, Pennsylvania

1989–1992

Yet when I surveyed all that my hands had done and what I had toiled to achieve, everything was meaningless, a chasing after the wind; nothing was gained under the sun.
(Ecclesiastes 2:11)

Twenty-five

the angst of youth
        is that
I cannot feel angst
because I am too young.
thirtysomething so real to me
        and yet
I am five years away
from that pinnacle year.

As I sit

the sun warms my cat
        as I sit
                and define myself

editing, singing
always giving
sometimes dreaming
always yearning

the sun warms my cat
        as I sit
                and define myself

he knows better
than to put words to feelings

What is missing

What is missing
from this very crowded
very complicated
life?

I work but wonder
for whom
for what

> write
> sing
> paint
> yearn
> dream

Will it always be like this?

I am dying of boredom

Ennui* floods my soul
    clutches my heart

Terrifying need to do more
    to be more
The despair is real
    but intangible

I am bored
I am so bored
I am dying of boredom.

---

*en·nui [on wee]
    boredom from lack of interest: weariness and dissatisfaction with life that results from a loss of interest or sense of excitement.
[Mid-18th century. Via French from, ultimately, Latin *in odio*, in the phrase *in odio est* "it is hateful" (source of English annoy).]
—from the *Encarta* World English Dictionary*

Why this need for words?

Why this need for words?
Must we explain tonight's poetry

      smear paint to canvas
      pen words with no meaning
      sing no songs
      drive drive drive

It is 1990
      and we are still young tonight.

Stagnant waters

stagnant waters
residual feelings
the time has come
to part the waters
looking for the fresh springs
that surge below

Fire painting

Rhapsodies and melodies
      fantasias of red and black
      yellow drips and black streaks
      and red blood red life
colors scream and weave
      across the page

No soul without love

creative energies well up
to overflowing
this need to paint
      and sing
      and write all night
can be explained by the hormonal
surges of a young woman in love with life
with no one to love
we are merely ego and hormones
no soul without love.

The night is cool and dark

The night is cool and dark
(as all nights should be).
The breeze rustles through the golden leaves of a yonder tree.
A soul can be heard sighing. A heart can be heard singing.
The day is cool and dark
(as days should be occasionally).
The wind whirls around the golden leaves that have fallen from a tree.
A man can be heard crying. A harp can be heard playing.
A fantasy of dark cool nights and dark cool days
of wind and trees and leaves and music and
the dark is cool and night a breeze leaves a soul sighing
singing playing crying
man a leaves wind a and cool is day dark the dark soul
rustles yonder
heard golden hearts singing. golden harp a from fallen
and dark be can wind cool The cool dark golden yonder
cool dark golden sighing singing day
heart soul tree leaves breeze Night.
playing crying wind leaves tree man harp.

My greatest fear

My greatest fear is that I will be ordinary
So poignant my feelings are
until I learn
they have been felt before

I should be comforted
by this link to others
but I am embarrassed
by this lack of originality

My words comfort me tonight

my words comfort me tonight
they are true to me like no other
sing sing sing from my pen
to the souls of my reader
can it be that I am your singer, too
young men and young women
old men and old women
damaged hearts and fresh faces
do I sing only for you or only for me?

No Touch

a painful loneliness clutches
at my center of being
why so lonesome
with so many friends
no real affection
caresses missing from my day
oh to be loved
touched
touched again
muscles tense
clenched tight with stress
longing for hands
to loosen the chains
of no touch

Amen

a loss of confidence
a minor setback
major doubts
no job no man
why hang on
why so eager

detach

there's no hurry

don't be too eager

Amen.

I. To the Pharmacy

My prayer is the prayer of fulfillment

Why isn't Christ enough
Why aren't pretty clothes enough

Why must human love needed be
to combat this dreaded wretched ennui

Were I not myself aware
of Emma Bovary
I, too, might try the pharmacy

II. To the Pharmacy

Emma Bovary —
why are you
haunting me again?
Am I to join you
in your Catholic phase?
It would be better
than this longing
for man to fill the void.
Or shall I follow you
to the pharmacy?
No — we must try
the Catholic phase once more
before we try the
pharmacy again.
The cross it shall be!

It is Sunday
and the drugstore is closed.

the unbearable lightness of being

gray days spent dreamily
wrapped in your arms
electric blanket
cool draft
trucks roar by
oblivious to our love-spent bodies

if only to awaken my senses
it is enough
to have loved for one night

the unbearable lightness of being
I must re-read

I'm gonna laugh you outta my life

I'm gonna laugh you outta my life
the jazz singer croons
we are fools when we love
        and trust
                and have faith
                      in higher powers
It's all a lie, I cannot express
the disappointment
*I'm gonna laugh you right outta my life
and no one will know you broke my heart*
such poetry she sings
while I pass the time
until I am disappointed again

No expectations

no expectations
no delusions

I simply work
  and write
  and sing
  and paint

no desires
no rejections

Must I sit in the sunbeam?

Like the Virgin Mary
must I sit in the sunbeam
and wait for the impregnation
      for the Annunciation
Must I wait like the Holy Mother
      for my life to bear fruit?
Must her way be my way
Do I really have no control of my destiny
Can I live without trying to force success
      from my career
           my quest for joy
           my pursuits of higher knowledge?

"O rest in the Lord
      wait patiently for Him
      and He shall give thee thy heart's desires.
Commit thy way unto him, and trust in Him
      and fret not thyselves because of evil doers.
O rest in the Lord
      wait patiently for Him
      and He shall give thee thy heart's desires."

I sing my favorite Mendelssohn aria
      and forget to embrace its truth.
Hail, Mary, full of grace
You are a better woman than I.

I must be strong and wise

From where does this strength come
this inner drive to live
despite God's teasing
I will defy His setbacks.
He is testing me,
they say I can't understand yet
because it is His will.

His will pulls — my will pulls.
I won't be defeated.
I won't be teased.
I won't be fooled again.
I cannot keep hopes high in this world.
Perhaps in the next I may hope and dream.
But in this life I must be strong and wise.
Not unfeeling but not expecting too much.

joie de vivre

joie de vivre
a joy
a delight in being alive
God's presence
shown at last
a ray of hope
a glimmer of truth
a wellness
a satisfaction
a vessel being filled
bursting with joy
and Thanksgiving
Alleluia

A hopeful time

November and sunshine pours
through the window
blessing my cat and me
such warmth is a gift at
this time of year
golden warmth
      leaves
      sunshine
      piano keys gilded by long
      fingers gliding
      a hopeful time
      a yearning for peace
      as summer continues well into fall.

I. Ennui grips again

an exasperation that knows no end
ennui grips again
a lackluster life
that shines as though full
why does everyone think I'm okay

II. Ennui grips again

ennui grips again
too bored to even drink or smoke or fetch chocolate
from the store

too bored to cry or scream or pray
must I live with myself

Stasis in darkness

It is night
my body aches
with longing
for the ennui
to be gone

Stasis in darkness
my friend Sylvia said

Sylvia Anne Virginia*
I cry to you
do we writer women
have to die

my womb wanders
wonders
empty tonight

* *Sylvia Plath, Anne Sexton, Virginia Woolf*

Hanging On

I'm hanging on
by
just a thread
my scissors
are
poised
I'm
ready
to
snip

I try to sing

I try to sing but
I can't even take
a deep breath of late
what darkness surrounds
my lungs and heart
I feel so empty
yet too full
to take a breath

God hear my cry my cry my cry my cry
why can't I cry or sing tonight

Wailing virgins

I cry the cry of the
      wailing virgins
      moaning in the night
      my body is empty
      tonight the tears won't come.

God, it's late

God, it's late
too late for joy
just numbness will do
I don't expect miracles
I will not blame my father

Runaway

my cat chases shadows
on the wall
perhaps he has found
my soul
I fear she has
run away from home

I feel too much now

the stoicism of my youth
is gone
I feel too much now
no liquor in the house
to numb the pain
five days until payday

Sweet wine symphony

The wine is warm
nighttime glistens
airplane murmur
sweet wine symphony
a song of nighttime harmony
red and sweet and tender
the wine is warm
nighttime haunts
the memory
of one sweet and dear to me
plays on

Excuse me

Excuse me,
I am searching for my soul.
I believe she wandered out
while I was busy
doing other things.

Words of truth

words of truth
are often
inexplicably so
ask any mother
who has looked
into the eyes
of her newborn
dripping with blood
moist and dirty
truth speaks
to the soul

The Birthing

a mother and
> daughter
> breathe
> as one
> then slowly
> pull away
> sometimes
> ripping out
> the heart
> of each other
> before the
> birthing is done

CHESTER SPRINGS, PENNSYLVANIA

1992

"Meaningless! Meaningless!" says the Teacher.
"Utterly meaningless! Everything is meaningless!"
(Ecclesiastes 1:2)

*An Orchid in the Arctic**

One careless footstep

the orchid
>lost a petal
>>tonight

years of nurture
>lost
>>with
>>>one careless
>>>footstep

No room for mystery and magic

how to argue
with the educated
the academics
know it all
no room
for mystery and
magic

they are not
random samplings

denial runs deep

There is a profound difference

There is a profound difference
between
the Orchid
and
the Arctic

The Orchid
understands
without statistics
The Arctic
needs proof

It is so lonely in the Arctic

it is so lonely
in the Arctic
they do not realize
how cold it is
they think we are
hysterical because
our theories cannot
be proven

Orchids' Haven

we need a place
to bloom and grow
warm and dark
and sunny and
moist where
we will not
be stepped on
trampled to death
by the oppressors
they are often
within

Orchid Truth

the random samples
are not the Truth
or even proven theories
we know what is true
because it rings
in the heart
we are often cold

*written with the inspiration of Kay Leigh Hagan, author of
"Orchids in the Arctic: The Predicament of Women Who Love Men"

I want to smear pink paint

I want to smear
pink paint
on the walls
rub my femininity
into the cracks
purple on the ceiling
red on the floor
black as night
smeared into the curtains
desecrate the sacred
sanctify the profane
paint paint paint

The Holy Grail

the wish for revenge eats up my soul
as I try to define my needs
I need to act on my rage
I have daydreams
of boxing
        target practice with big guns
        blowing up people with a machine gun
        stabbing my father over and over again
        slaying dragons in a dark forest
When do I get to the Holy Grail?

little tiny shards of glass

little tiny shards of glass
piercing through my skin
little tiny shards of glass
buried in my heart like gold
knives
sharp
shards
glass
cut
pain
pinpoints of blood
pick them out one by one

Shattered

my trust
shattered
like tiny shards
of glass
my heart lies
in little pieces
on the floor

Wild women

wild women
laughing old crones
cackle into the night
the others
will never
understand
our power

A woman sings

A woman sings
(but it ain't always pretty)
feet apart
breathing deep
head held high
she breathes music into life
she moans of deep rivers and longs for new places
she croons for lost lovers and scorns pretty faces
she shouts for joy bought with pain
she's lived amazing graces.

A woman sings
(but it ain't always for Truth)
the dresses
the glitter
the lights
the gaze upon her
she opens her mouth to sing
the air fills her as she fills the room with her soul
and then the songs
fill the air and the hearts of the people.

The applause is the very best of all.

WEST PLAINS, MISSOURI

1994–1995

*Can a mother forget the baby at her breast
and have no compassion on the child
she has borne? Though she may forget,
I will not forget you.*
                  (Isaiah 49:15)

I am a new mother

Peace. Tranquility.
A babe in arms.
A cloud floats by my window.
The leaves fall softly.
I am a new mother.
All is well.
My baby is safe and warm.

Sylvia, I'm sorry

I thought I understood Sylvia Plath until today
but
I am a mother now.

Sylvia, I loved you.
I thought I knew you.
I, too, have lived in a bell jar.

I admired you for your courage
but
now I see you were really a coward to kill yourself
you couldn't face the music
of your imperfection in life
so you concocted
the Perfect death.

Why did you do it?
How could you leave your babies that way?
I hate you for wanting to be so perfect.
I hate that part of me.
She makes me tired with her incessant complaining.

I cannot imagine killing myself and leaving my daughter
on her own
to live with her mother's legacy of perfectionism.

Sylvia, I'm sorry,
but I think I'll choose life today, though, I, too, often
contemplate death. Perhaps it's time for me to try to be less
perfectionistic.
Or, at least, less suicidal.

It's about time

Mother, why didn't you teach me things?
How come I never knew you?
Where were you when it happened?
Why didn't you stop him?
How can you say you love me?
Why did you let me cry?
Why did you even have children?
Why are you so unhappy?
Why don't you do something about anything?
Why are you so weak? (I used to think you were strong)
Why can't I forgive you?
Why are you jealous of me? (aren't parents supposed to
want their children to have more than they did as children?)
Why are you crying now?
I needed your sympathy then.
Oh, you're crying because you feel guilty.
Good. It's about time.

WEST PLAINS, MISSOURI

1999

For I am convinced that neither death nor life, neither angels nor demons, neither the present nor the future, nor any powers, neither height nor depth, nor anything else in all creation, will be able to separate us from the love of God that is in Christ Jesus our Lord.
(Romans 8:38-39)

For the love of God

Why don't I believe in the love of God?
If my parents didn't love me, why should God?
I am not lovable. My sins are too great.
What was my sin?
Vulnerability. I trusted in my father. I craved my
mother's love.
    love me
    love me
    love me
I needed them to love me, but it was not to be.
They were proud of me. I performed so well in school.
At home they said I was a little devil, and I believed.
I learned not to need too much. Applause became enough.
When the applause died down, I performed some more.
The audience loves me.

Were You There

Were you there when they crucified my Lord?
I sing and sing and sing and wonder, God
Were you there when my daddy took my soul?
Just believe. He answers prayers.
Why should I believe in a God who cannot stop abusers
from hurting little children.
They tell me You are love, God.
If You love me, why didn't You protect me?
You let your own son hang on a cross, why should I
believe You'd do any different for me.
God protects even the smallest sparrow they say.
Yes, I've seen them gutted by cats.
Pretty comforting God, He is.
My head believes Your Word, but my heart does
not yet trust You.

WEST PLAINS, MISSOURI

2000

*Much dreaming and many words are meaningless.
Therefore stand in awe of God.*
                    (Ecclesiastes 5:7)

bad poetry

I must write some bad poetry
get these creaky brain cells
back in gear.
I love the white paper
the pens.
I love my computer, too,
Sleek and black, it beckons.
Tap my keys. Watch the letters careen across the page.

Poetry. Bad poetry. Who cares.
I am writing again.
Ink splashes across
the page. The letters dance
across the screen.

Oh, alphabet, I am yours!

So sweet to write again!

the screen doesn't lie

poets don't write poems on the computer
so sue me
sometimes I do
sometimes I love to watch the words careen
across the screen
pen to paper is sometimes too close
to the body
too hot to the touch
the computer lets me see before I feel
safer
cleaner
neater
freer
no attachment to the feelings
no problem
no poems
no paper and pen, but yes yes yes yes yes to poetry
yes, I am a poet
the screen doesn't lie

my heart is singing

I am I am I am I am
a poet
      poet
      poet
      poet
I will not deny it any longer
my heart is singing
"I knew it all along" she says
how could I deny my deepest longings
and call myself a communicator of
the importance of dreams
fake coach fake coach fake coach fake coach
my muse screamed
with good reason
if I am to communicate love and
the importance of following our dreams
guess I'd better follow my own
      bliss
      bliss
      bliss
      bliss
I am I am I am I am
a poet
      poet
      poet
      poet

bliss bliss bliss

I imagine the poets
who do not use computers
to ply their craft
are terrified
of letting the screen
devour their words.
slow down slow down
slow down slow down
slow down slow down
why slow down?
I am so elated at discovering my
bliss bliss bliss!
I'll type as fast
as I want to

melting

today I declare myself
free to write
whatever
comes out of me
melting
I am a writer
published not yet
but not to worry
we can turn on that side
of the brain
whenever needed
for now
we need to turn on the heart
frozen
by my need
to find a nice way
to make lots of money
my heart needs to melt
again
melt
into the poet

West Plains, Missouri

2001

*The fear of the Lord is the beginning of wisdom,
and knowledge of the Holy One is understanding.*
(Proverbs 9:10)

September 11, 2001

tragedy
terror
television
trade centers
pentagon
pennsylvania
torn asunder.
the very heart of me
torn asunder, too
1200 miles away
I search amidst the rubble
bearing buckets of ash and metal
looking for survivors
from the destruction of my soul.
all I find is bitter tears and waves of sadness
no survivors but me
my mother is dead
my father is dead
I survive for what end?
for my husband
and our children
I have been given life.
yes, for them, but what about me?
while
a part of me hungers for the ultimate rest
resentful of those who breathe no more,

another part of me screams
for breath to live alive and lively.
I write poems
because creativity matters
even more now.
the rest can wait
while I create my life.

learning to love is just the beginning

in all I do I fail
trying to prove I am worthy
worthy of the love I crave.

what if I am not worthy
but I choose to love
myself anyway?

will it matter if I love
myself?

love does not seem real
coming from myself.

another's love would heal,
but whose love is eternal?

God is love, they say, but
who wants love
that does not protect
or keep safe?

How can I trust Him?

WEST PLAINS, MISSOURI

2002

Shout for joy, O heavens; rejoice, O earth;
burst into song; O mountains!
For the Lord comforts his people and will have
compassion on his afflicted ones.
                              (Isaiah 49:13)

but I am not God

it seems the rain will never end
thunder   lightning   swollen creeks
drought ended
floods beginning
I don't mean to be rude
but it seems God
is not very logical

if I were God
I think I'd make a
lovely shower occur
at midnight
everywhere
everyday
a few inches of rain
per week
each week
no one inconvenienced
except perhaps for
an occasional nurse or night clerk
cursing the rain on her way
to work
most people, though, would
enjoy the sound of nightly
rain on their roof

Shout for Joy

sun up
dry up
the roads
and grassy fields
ready for business
everyone gets enough rain that way
but I am not God

motherhood, millions, matters

Dear God,

I am restless again.
Home with the children.
Career on hold.
What do you want me to do?

so what if motherhood were your
main career right now.
what better material for writing
than time with your children?
go write poetry

Ha, for no salary I went to Bryn Mawr!
Ha, for no salary I was outstanding biz school grad!
pass the coffee to the writer-mommy
me and my kids at the Ozark Café
I'm going to write some books

writer-mommy, you laugh, JK Rowling's worth millions!

ok, ok, ok
maybe I could be JK Rowling of the Ozarks.
novel writing can be lucrative,
but poetry?
no way.

*Why did you ask Me for help
if you weren't going to listen
to My answer?*

because I didn't think you would tell me
to write poetry!

*poetry
poetry
poetry
write it
creativity matters
creativity matters
creativity matters*

dear God, what's this nonsense all about?
I think I'll stop praying now.

intentional life

intentional life
eyes on True North
my North Star
>loving
>kindness
>forgiveness
>Jesus Christ
>resurrected

intentional life
eyes on True North
while my natural
inclination
is due South
>unloving
>unkind
>unforgiving
>selfish
>boastful
>dead

intentional life
eyes on True North
never knowing it all
but knowing enough
to keep walking

toward my final
destination
    Jesus Christ
    resurrected
    living
    calling
    my name

divorce

my heart torn out
and handed to me
on a silver platter
we'll still be friends
you said
friends?
my friends do not
treat me this way
I still love you
you said
love?
love is patient
      kind
      never boastful
      nor rude
you are boastful
      rude
      lying
      lying
      lying
friends?
love?
go find yourself another
fool

aftermath

so many things
that were we
are now just
me

everything
cut in half
split apart
right down
the middle

the kids
the stuff
the money
the house
my heart

like one
whose mate
has a long
lingering
illness
I've already
said goodbye

we stopped
being we
a very long
time ago

for years
it's just
been
me and
the kids

you have
been
alone
for a very long
time

and will be
for a long
time to come

glimmer of joy

joy is elusive
ennui ever-present
doubts fill my heart
I am tired of the journey

JOY JOY JOY
I shout for you
I search for you
amidst the ruins
of my broken heart

JOY JOY JOY
I shout for you
I search for you
I see you now
there, inside the chaos
lies joy undisturbed

joy was there all along
I just had to shout in pain
for her to know
I believed in You
and Your saving grace
JOY JOY JOY
you are but a glimmer

but you are there
hopeful, shimmering

today, I rejoice in the
light dancing on water
leaves blowing in the wind
my children swinging
oblivious to the shouts of pain
that birthed my joy
their daddy doesn't love me

JOY JOY JOY
I have shouted for you
I have searched for you
and there you are
waiting for me
and my embrace

today I hold joy's hand
as my heart
cries in pain
I shout for joy
as I continue
on the journey again.

SPRINGFIELD, MISSOURI

2003

Shout for joy to the Lord, all the earth.
Worship the Lord with gladness;
come before him with joyful songs...
For the Lord is good and his love endures forever...
(Psalm 100: 1-2, 5a)

thanks, God

Write poetry!

thanks, God.
so sorry I asked You for advice.
are You crazy?
me, write poetry?
that's an efficient way to make money!
how can I call myself a coach dedicated to helping people find their most efficient way to make money and then You call me to write poetry. I looked to You to help me find a nice way to make money and You're telling me to write poetry?

What if you dedicated your career to helping people find what really matters?
like poetry
pottery
painting
small children
sunsets
singing

Wait a minute, God!
I thought I needed money for what matters? How can I feed the poor if I don't make money?

*The poor will always be with you.
Write poetry!
Feed their souls and you feed Me.
Pour your poetry on My feet
and wash them with your hair.
Rub your words between My toes
and caress the rough places with
your metaphors.
My people need your poetry.
Your poems will coach My people
in finding their own way of
honoring me.
When you write you will feel My
pleasure.
Do it for Me
and the poor will be fed.*

Daddy?

*God tries to read the newspaper,
but His little girl has big questions.*

Daddy?
Yes, my child?
Are You really God?
Yes.
Am I really Your child?
Yes.
Daddy?
Yes, my child.
Does that make me a goddess?
No, you are My princess.
Then am I really a diva, daddy?
Do you like to sing? Do you like the bright lights?
Yes, Daddy.
Do you like it when the angels smile?
Yes, Daddy.
Do you love the applause?
Yes, Daddy.
Does it make you smile?
Yes, Daddy.
Then, you, My child, are a diva.
Daddy?
Yes, my child.
Do You still love me?
Yes, my child.
Even though I'm a diva?

Yes, My child. I will always love you.
Even when I pretend to be a goddess?
Yes, My child.
I made your love for the stage and the stars.
Just promise Me one thing.
What Daddy?
Don't ever forget who made you
and why I want you to sing.
Why do You want me to sing, Daddy?
When you sing, it gives Me pleasure.
Thank You, Daddy. I am Your diva.
You're welcome. Now go play so I can read the paper.
Yes, Daddy.

die editor die

red red red red pen
editor's blood seeps
across the page
of my life

red red red red pen
I am editing
as I go
through this life

red red red red pen
bleed bleed bleed
my words
will come to life

despite my
best intentions

thirty-nine

thirty-nine
almost 40
the angst of youth gone
second act of my life
about to begin

can it be 20 years
since I left home
and the safety
of your arms?

I look back
on my journey
so many regrets
so many wasted years
      away from home
      away from you
      away from God

letting you go
seeking adventure
I simply endured
I nearly succumbed to
      the ennui
      the city streets
      too many temptations

I felt no love
      for God
      from God
Too many years away from home
I often longed for you

almost 40
I rejoice
you found me
I found you
"*amazing grace*
how sweet the sound
that saved a wretch like me
I once was lost but
now am found"
thirty-nine
and I am home
beginning anew
ennui has turned to joy

shout for joy

shout for joy
shout for joy
shout for joy
    alleluia
shout for joy
shout for joy
shout for joy
    praise the Lord
sing simply sing
the mysteries
we sought to
unravel
are simply
accepted
the truth is revealed
we've already won
the battle
the heart
rules the intellect
the sun continues
to shine
I am back in Missouri
and life is still difficult
but the Lord is still good

Bibliography & Notes

Encarta World English Dictionary* [North American Edition] © & (P)2004 Microsoft Corporation. All rights reserved. Developed for Microsoft by Bloomsbury Publishing Plc.

Niemeyer, Jonathan. *Harvesting Spiritual Fruit: Following God's Path to True Love, Joy and Peace.* Fairfax, Virginia: Xulon Press, 2002.

NIV Women of Faith Study Bible, New International Version. Grand Rapids, Michigan: Zondervan Publishing House, 2001.

Many years ago I came across a copy of an article, *"Orchids in the Arctic: The Predicament of Women Who Love Men,"* written by Kay Leigh Hagan. I have been unable to locate the source or the exact publication date, but it was a very intriguing look at gender differences.

About the Author

Born in Chicago in 1964 to a Sicilian immigrant and an aspiring painter, Sharina Smith moved to Missouri in 1970 and was raised on a small farm in the Ozarks milking goats, sheering sheep, and building barns in which she would one day be abused. Sharina endured her abusive childhood by writing poetry, reading, singing, and dreaming of life in the big city. At the age of eighteen, Sharina realized her dream of escaping to the city by securing a scholarship to Bryn Mawr College where she graduated in 1986. She continued her education at West Chester University of Pennsylvania and enjoyed a career in the business world. Sharina has come full circle and resides again in the Missouri Ozarks with her husband, Chuck, and their combined family of four children. Sharina is now a poet, writer, singer, and serves full-time in the worship and music ministry of her church.

Sharina is always honored to hear from her readers. Please write to her directly at:
    2825 Springfield Farms Blvd., #250
    Brookline Station, MO 65619

For more information, see www.sharinasmith.com.

The Servant Song:
poems from the shadows

In her next collection of poetry, Sharina Smith explores her role as servant to her Lord, her husband, her children, her church, and her readers. She also looks at the theme of shadows in our lives, in music, in paintings, and in literature:

> *in the shadows*
> *we are born*
> *we are called to live*
> *we are called home*
> *we are resurrected*

Printed in the United States
18810LVS00003B/151-198